Be[yond]

Sarah James

To John with thanks for the buddying! Sarah James

NEWTON-LE-WILLOWS

Published in the United Kingdom in 2013
by The Knives Forks And Spoons Press,
122 Birley Street,
Newton-le-Willows,
Merseyside,
WA12 9UN.

ISBN 978-1-909443-21-1

Acknowledgements:

Thanks are due to the editors of the websites and magazines where versions of the following poems have been published previously or are forthcoming: 'Reading Aloud with My Son' on the R.A.S.P. (Rebelling Against Spelling Press) website; 'Broken' in *streetcake* magazine; 'Home Remedy for a Broken Heart' on *Ink, Sweat and Tears*; 'Betrayal' in *Abridged*, 'Composition' in *Sculpted: Poetry of the North West*. 'The (un)bespoken' was created as part of the Manchester Metropolitan University/Royal Philharmonic Society 'Notes into Letters' project.

Cover Art: Sam Hutchcocks and Julie Haller of Moonlit Murals (www.moonlitmurals.net)

Table of Contents

From Earth and Fire

Against Air and Water

Skin on Water

This only in the first instance. After immersion, temperature settles, selves disintegrate, the distance between cells equates. Stillness falls. Not as the apple from a tree, not a wrestler floored, not eyelids in sleep. As a candle-flame-beyond-draughts shadows wax on cave walls. Concentrated hypnosis. Unflickered.

This water's wick wears no skin. It skims the body as a pebble, smooths separated perception. Everything curves within. Even the nerves' gut-tautened harp strings, yearning for the shape of a cello.

All this while air still vibrates around. Strum. Hum. The occasional notes unstrung.

So the force lure of amniotic memory away. Until peace reaches perturbance in flesh made for motion.

Ants, wasps, spiders – all kick against the inevitable sink surge to one flow, resist perpetuity's wet vessels.

Slick, slick, laps the lake of thoughts at my hours' fingers. Thoughts eddy, unsteady slack gusts at fault's sails. Blame. Guilt. Doubt. Internal conflict.

With time, the unsure ground solidifies.

Water on Skin

No stripping is needed for contact to take place. Try in vain to stop atoms' jostle: solids vibrate, liquids will filter, gas passes ungrasped.

But open the mouth, where sounds are wracked…bare teeth, the untied tongue and self-centred vowels obstruct the free movement of air.

Water bounces most speech. Waveforms speed, their wake sleeks. Edged by sand, rock, the grass roots of mud banks, and patterns of ceramic tiling, sounds re[verb]erate, shape-shifting. Only in air do spoken words flint.

But, all this aside, echoes lodge in us. And I am me, whatever that vibration means. If I ripped loose the seams, perhaps black would outflow. Or is it the dark bits that tack me in place – a trail of rivets that steel metal magma inside?

Nearly 1800 miles away, the earth mantles its smoulder around a core of hard iron.

Weight presses the world into me not me to the world.

When it rains, nerves welcome the touch. Layers slowly disappear. Synthetic fibres flatten to another skin, while cotton shrinks to new strength.

Solid masses, from liquid accumulations. Rain, river, sea-sucked, cloud-form, over-accumulation, more rain, extra river... water's many renditions. The faces of buildings say these days are acidic, that we've manufactured our ageing into their expressions.

For we are all older's kin, however we distance this, with pro-enzymic enhancers, anti-ebbtides and rejuvajunkitems: vanity is a flotsam. Narcissus bends still to kiss the water fixed in glass windows.

Identity distends, drenched by such reflections.

Mostly I dry without stain, other times mascara-wasted. Still, stone and flesh: dust particles gyrate.

Butterfly

No air creature in water, I adapt this position once only. More eel with splatter wings, snaking and churning. Water scatters electric splutters.

Pink/black/blue-capped matchsticks dunk around me: sparks of damp (un)lit along this line of fire.

But if the only giving is giving oneself whole-heartedly... To it: chrysalis-burst of stained glass windows; symmetry in parts; people in halves. The fast-stroked. The swift-flighted. And slower paths between: a petal splash, a sepal hiatus.

The eel's spiel, the serpent's long hiss enfolded in wet flesh, is by water silenced.

When I emerge, as some estranged half-grounded, half-liquid creature in what passes for reality (for want of firmer sounds), forked tongues drip, flat black against my face's paleness.

After I've changed, I reflect in the half-mirror, hair still cloying. Denial recoils, a hidden slithering inside.

I have never before met eyes which are lakes or skies, only pale-scaled blackness.

When he laughs, it's as one who knows how this means. Even the air rushes towards him.

The Wave Machine

That summer in Birmingham, a beach sprawls outside the library: all pop music and visual Bahamas jingles, surrounding deckchairs and dirty sand, dirty sand and deckchairs. The odd red bucket, even a plastic spade or two, abandoned.

The water, if there is water (I no longer remember), is not remarkable.

The sun is more seaside, promenaded in shop windows. Above them, vertical glass waves cemented in permanent tsunami.

This skyline higher than memory, the present noisier than the past, kerbs cry out for comfort. A confusion of faces convulses, crushes towards me. My guts contract. And re-pulse. Grab cold metal. Breathe!

I've arranged to meet him here somewhere, only I can't recall his exactitudes. If I clip my mind round the earhole, torture it for clues…only iron railings trickle and fragments of voices.

I circle back. To the bright T-shirt wasteland, city sand and rooftop trawlers. Ice-cream sludge. Wafer flakes: a Hansel trail, bated. Breadcrumbed-out, pigeons swipe up stray chips, shit everywhere. Breathe!

Hydrophobic

Some days are all elbows and thumbs. Then air makes me nervous. But also water. All the things that refuse to mix – or rest in stillness.

Bruises spread, away from their pain, beautiful in their surface iridescence: a black beetle shell exposed to light, oil pelted into a puddle, ermine sleek.

Lately, my silver-plated fear is greater than that which I can sprawl out along lined paper. Velvet-awed cutlery, it chinks everyday ceramics.

One evening, I'm treated to dinner out: tête-à-tête candles for two, or…thirteen tables laid and lit, wax rain falling. His head tipped towards his mobile.

Balsamic vinegar bubbles. Intergalactic dust clouds the gas around it: phobic sea of oil, white-dished, squared.

His neat nails are manicured inertness on a wine glass. Undipped, our non-daily bread: crusted slabs of soft marble veined with air, textured to soak up dark acidity and tang sparks on our tongues – if fingers break the whiteness to share.

We leave its basket untouched.

Metal sounds: knife, fork / spoon, fork brought together, parted, contact angled back again. The same vowels sitting down to dine in like mouths otherwise elsewhere in time. Clipped phrases.

Folded fabric. Linen edges slope to the laps' gentle thighs, unpleated, gathering breadcrumbs, spilt oil and slack words.

I brace myself for more; seek out soft curves with my tongue.

Beyond Melting

Snow is not a kind of water. Mostly it is cruel.

Much apparent softness comes with deception. On the ground, footprints mash others. What lies beneath, secreted, rises with time in tinges of yellow, brown, tarmac black.

In the air, it throws asterisks at my face. They hit aslant, as blunted hyphens. Flakes mascara-clog my upturned gaze, glaze weathered cheeks, push lips beyond redness. Hat, gloves, stance shape themselves around it. Skin dries in its pale eczema image.

Yes, this is the white stuff of past years' wonder.

And yet...sometimes still the pull of strange kinship. A reminder of substantial metamorphosis. Adaptations to, and fro.

Oxygen

H_2O is desiccated to not even the trace of a listing in my dictionary of art symbols. Undefined.

Elsewhere, what is everywhere, or almost, is in fact nowhere to be seen, in purity.

The wet saliva tongued to fingertip is electrolyted, mucussed, with glycoproteins, lysozymes, enzymes...

The swimming pool swallows me into chlorine, urine, (un)chemicalled discharge, flecks of strange bodies.

Tap water quenches with its own aqua cocktail of chlorine, fluorosilicic acid, aluminium sulphate, calcium hydroxide, a little sodium silicofluoride. Maybe salts of arsenic, radium, aluminium, copper... Hormones, nitrates and pesticide contaminants.

Add an ice-cube, or heat and caffeinate the mix.

Or pressurize with extra flavourings siphoned into squat metal. Place its touch-sized curves in a hand, design a sexy slogan, the brandings of canned desire: expectant, figure of eight at a slant, mouth pushed open, silvered tongue sliver tucked sharply downwards away from the space of flow: E150d-phosphoric-liquid-caramel-acid-air-sugar-fizzing...

Vases stagnate flower stems, dull clarity's semblance.

Plant roots sip – ionic proportions and bicarbonate anion. They thrive/writhe on liquidised acidic gases.

Yet still, from toxicity, their leaves (re-)generate: oxygen.

Wholly trinities re-form: CO_2 H_2O

air-shy, water-dry

'the assumption of the armour of an alienating identity' – Jacques Lacan

there's a name for you, Narcissus nymph,
you dumb-stuck, up-smiled, sucked bitch!

there's names for you, water-knickered slut, love,
should of bin a stripper, slap-struck dump-fuck

who'd name for you? dried vase on the side,
fat, brown-leafed bride, unthorned wife

find a name for that, brass slipper, Ophelia-laked,
glass-faced, cheek mother…snigger!

there was a name for you, hen-peck turkey,
bloated goat, bleating sow, silt-eared cow-bleed

here's a name for you, other, Other, society-sized,
mirror-myth me, Me ME!

'From the bottom of the pool, fixed stars' – Sylvia Plath, 'Words'

err chide, watered wry

Beyond Tilting

After water has chucked itself at the house for some space-time beyond the counted metres of the mind's days, I find my black hat, pull his coat from its hook and open the door.

Outside. Cold shoves. Shock scratches my eyes. Life gusts towards me: colours, shapes, noise.

I hug the wool's heaviness, pull its rough thickness close at the neck, feel its hugeness without him.

Fabric hunches, air pleats around me. Water sidles across pavements, arcs out of gutters, slumps into mud and grass.

And there is the wet where he parked the car, the tyre-troughed edge, the place of his last wave, that kiss which slid from my cheek to fall…where did it fall that day of not-rain? Where is the fall before day, the dayfall before, the foreday befall, the before fallday, the…

How slow that pace which measures from there to here, from the door to the end of the drive, the drive to somewhere undriven, to anywhere unriven…if I angle my neck, try to precise that last tilt of his face towards me…

Looking up now, a splash of blue corners the street. My neighbour approaching, his arm raised to wave.

Ambushed, the flesh of my fingers replies without me. So far away still, the fact of my hand.

Nearer, dead leaves cling to my shoes. There, the space where he would have raked them. Have. Raked. Them. Wood.

Un(Synchronised)

Loneliness greets me at the Ericeira shell's mouth. My mock fisherman's shack empty, I rattle in its stone vastness; too small to raise a lasting echo.

Down from the cliff-
drop, surf hurls noise at the rocks, breaks its own scalloped mosaics, as it contours shoreline ridges.

Linked-hand, two strangers on the sand's ebbing heat. Their feet pattern makeshift paths ahead of the tide.

A child runs after.

No sign of the rivers which sourced this palette.

Evening light folds to night ocean. Leaving my portholed outlook to stand alone on the beach, my brittle-boned frame shrinks in its soft enamel, and colder black left by the blue's wake. My stars here set so far asunder – last splashes of light in a sky that's dried-up.

I skim a shell at the waves.

Darkness engulfs it. I imagine its echoes, drowning, as the sea reclaims its emptiness.

Blue

The missing of a person is the strangest space. The missing of several forces similarities.

I discover places beyond, past accumulations.

But loneliness exists as a feeling by itself.

Blue has many shades, this much is obvious. Until the edges merge. Like the little I know. All eyes are not the same, it would seem. An Inuit white unlikely to match my bleached landscapes. Or the contrasts created by its colours.

Blues I have borrowed thus far include the ragged hem of his jeans. That christening of ribbons around my first son's crib. The bruises I see, unlike those which are hidden. The rainbow's giving way to rich purples. Never the sky but often the sea, though aquamarine encroaches.

But always those points when something catches the mind, when I stop watching and time sharpens to a needle – threads slip through the eye.

With me, without me, the clock's hands pierce crimson wormholes. In life as we know it, love, only as little as we know it.

I knot those I have as secure as I can, concentrate on the beauty of each delicate stitch, not the whole unreeling. And sometimes then, a space arises from the deep; a moment's grace where I forget to measure. Movement happens without me. My body threads. The universe glistens with beads.

Through the Ether

Graven

Bodies loll and roll against
arc of her spine, laughter rushing.
His words on her tongue
disowned jealousy. In this
bricked lobe, slugs of rain
unclogging, coiled thoughts,
stirring air, in and out.
He still cracks at her shell
sometimes. It's said later,
a fleeting hoped escape
patches. As blue bruises,
breath disappears, sucked
into choked-tail, snaked hiss.

Poem In Which Mouse is Seen Not He(a)rd

As if the scratch of her mouth
once opened

might let the soul rush out
in a gush of red

vowels, unspooling
those blood-written

family rules cogged tight
in unspoken tradition.

Silence
spliced into crossed genes.

Only, the cat that's got her tongue –
pressed to flat pe(t)al

between the thin leaves
of their black-leathered Bible,

where Thomas begat father begat brothers
as Adam begat Seth begat Enos –

teaches her the art of claws;
that scratches will bleed.

Reading Aloud with My Son

Sum times **dis**tract his patter**ns**
   of th**ough**t **bl**ack fault lines
re**shape** the teacher's neat **page**

with multi**ply**inginging fract ures
Numbers crin**k**le until our e**ye**s
even out these un**scrip**ted odd**iti**es.

Just so, at st**or**ytime, when words
unruffle, loo**se-w**inged,
from the books sp**read** before him.

His 'd's buz**zzz** into fl**i**ght as bees;
letters c**law**, their beaks lur**ch**,
feathers uns**croll**. C**rows** scatter

in squiggles he can**not** tame
into a c**lear**, page-b**ound**, vision.
Only my vo**i**ce to th**read** tales

from **their** dizzy-e**ye**d cawing.

Draining

The sink's stainless steel waste,
punched holes which have let
water free-fall in one long white-noise.

Its flow forced to air bubbles, a star
spreading from the impact. Away

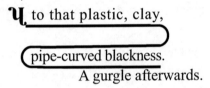 to that plastic, clay,

pipe-curved blackness.
                    A gurgle afterwards.

      Left behind – metal scratches,   pink
ice-cream fluorescence,   onion curves,
    loosed sweetcorn teeth,   something strange
    shredded…   & a single
    dark hair,

could be his, could be mine:
an arced line clinging to wet dross.

Betrayal

An empty can
grows two ring-pulls
in the train window, poised
open-winged in a parallel world.

There too, the gap left
by a metal tongue pushed down.

Into this thin-silvered darkness:

dried flesh, taste of stale fizz,
tide-marked lips –

that waking to the red of a known mouth
to find another's echo has crawled in,
embedded its forked hiss
into numbed silence.

From Archaeological Digs

Unmown grass arches over an autumn leaf;
its serrated wafer edges, points softening
into an unfinished rainbow of browns.
This diseased mottling to hen feathers,
a fortune teller's tea blend for the future.

How does this ageing work:
the next Neuropteris hollandica
preserved from these Renoir patterns?
Our child's play caught in foxy words
or written into fern seed fossils!

Living remembrance ungardened,
I grasp its wet stalk. History blades
my hand, as I lift this not-yet-earth
from green skies. Into the chill
shadowing my world now.

Air dries the leaf. Dullness pinched
between flesh and nail, I return it
new to old soil. The rain's stilled
acidic glass taints my fingers
with its changing transparency.

Which fragments – metal skin,
white teeth – will future's children pull
from the ground while neoprene
grass whistles on their lips?
Past vibrations beyond them.

For Granted

air **thrilling** a bare shoulder
sun worn without **glass**
the **mouth** as a **cataract**
a **river**'s steep descent, unferned
words
plunging **pulsing playing**
rebelling revolting revelling
revealing
no **hunched** bells pealing
nights framed only by **home** ground's **re-turning**
that **choice** to shun or clip
the metal **circles** made
from our fingers' **need** to fasten
the **shape** of daisy chains

*Rug*ged **Language**

matted **fray**, corn-ea(red)
tats of brown antennae
windbl(adder)ed surf **(a)mid**-curl
before **crash** (ef)fluenced f/led
how it (w)**edges**
off the **beat**(end)om
floor(s) **flat**(lines) **worn** (w)here
our **thread**/**tread**/breath
(g)rates again(st) **weight**
& yet **still** **exp.ands** **upwards** (encro)aches
in **its** **strand(ed)** **unweaving**
(in)finite p-p-p-**pulsed**
sing(le) **t/rack(s)** **(/)** **lungness**

Slap-Dash

pointless   dart
black mark   opening
a   line   in   space middle
slap   in   white
trace   of   semantics
semaphoric   brace
cummerbund &   belted
slip-sledge of penned ink
hyphened-out   in   texts
bookends   inverted
pauses   shelved
hanging   thoughts
postponement of purpose
a   crossword   gap
linking up   acrostics
division of some parts
afterwards fragmented
adjunct   advised
horizontal   front
flat on   1's   back
haphazard   sign
pulled   ap-art – ed.

R.E.M.

buckled belt – Orion's night
clip-on   stars – tinsel   tails – mermaid's   slit
knuckled   heart – flitting   tides – moon   stride
swarm   kisses – split   hives – allergic   knives
thrown   light – dream   silver – strewn   scream
short   shift – sharp   drifted – snow   wiles
flaked   smiles – slipped   red – thread   slipped
eyed   tight – lashed   light – slighted   strike
flash   bolt – iron   rivet – spoon   striped
hilt   holed – tilt   flies – hair   webbed
tint   sails – slip-on   cars – night   onions
buck   bolted – luck   slashed – splash   eyes
matted   black – might   dream – will   powered
caught feather – threaded kite – streamed meme
rooms unseam

Broken

& life's many caveats

...a thought of you,
our mapping incomplete
every time we come close

cells still recycle
demis to dermis
deep-gened to epi-
pigment to pigment

air-skimming
butterfly of muscles
swimming

give shape to a mouth
soothe creases from letters
across a face
trace [of] faults
shush...
fingers to lips whisper

shush!

Every touch is

Every touch is...

shush!
fingers to lips whisper
shush...

trace [of] thoughts
across a face
soothe creases from letters
give shape to a mouth

swimming
butterfly of muscles
air-skimming

pigment to pigment
deep-gened to epi-
dermis to dermis
cells still recycle
every time we come close
our mapping incomplete

...a thought of you,

& life's many caveats

Home Remedy for a Broken Heart

She knocked back one Sauvignon
bottle, two double vodka shots,
three G and Ts, HICCUPPED.
Four Bloody Marys
blurred tastebuds,
FIVE FLAMING
the smell of sick,
SAMBUCAS:
Six Singapored Slings saw her giggling sex –
'n flinging Basstardss! Seven somesing
BROKE HER NEW HEELS.
Ate, sorry, meant eight,
her tumble
arms helped to a taxi. Nine, no ten –
or was it eleven? – fingers swayed,
zen slumped in her lap.
There were more on her back!
And what about her face?
Darkness.
Twelve heads pillowed – vice-caught –
swung. Thirteen minutes' forgetting.
Before the cure fell <u>flat</u>.

Unread Book

Memory pleats on a kilt,
as the paperback thwacks
to the joists. A past present.
~~Retrieved from floored rafters.~~

et une fois, il est revenu me voir

Behind the squiggle of a man,
~~that book cover first impression,~~
a neat dedication: blue love,
dated. No Scottish s(h)lurred lilt.

là, où la cloche sonnait noir

But the aged space between
~~— yellowed/cliché of a page —~~
reels with tartan laughter,
ale-slicked cobbles, the stillness

de la lune, un lac sans allumettes

of Rouen's night fountains, a boot
detached from its heel, looped
bruises of keeling tunes,
~~tunes keeling in bruised loops,~~

la jeunesse danse devant les oubliettes

~~plastic soles tapping on laminate,~~
laddered tights, that spiral
of metal rungs ascending,
the gaps between revealing

avant la glisse, la fenêtre ouverte

> the empty room below, discarded
> ~~clothes…from the mind's folds,~~
> strangeness. Afterwards, my red-
> cheeked resting on that wolfish chest.

> *après la perte, la présence découverte*

> Later, *Le Loup des Steppes* – a moment
> balanced on temporary shelf edge,
> ~~held open in a hand, then closed,~~
> lodged back into a bookcase, ferried

les plumes du vol dans la bouche

> to and from an attic. White-
> spined, author/title on red/brown,
> ~~its pages mostly untouched, unturned,~~
> slotted now below *Blindsight*.

> *une chair de pluie où je me couche*

> Set back slightness between the *Tiger's
> Wife* and *The Toddlers Bible*. Translation
> of a translation of…

---

sans mots, trop tard la reconnaissance
> wordless, time rephrases past absence

d'or – of/from gold echoes

with thanks to David Hart and Worcester Cathedral Poets

i)   or   oR   OR
            the voice   in haloes
        its gold rim   curved   to the walls
    meaning   a 'simple'   opening   of doors

            today's   arbitrary   arch
        where I rest   my head   in stone
            an outer   ossicle
        with martyred   language   bones

        & there is   no knowing
                but the arc   of thoughts
            that startle   of touched flesh   on dreams
        this sun's   strange   solidities

            how even   the air
            has invisible   ores

ii)
                                aurora

            the voice   sin haloes

      its gold rink curved   to the waltz

meaning   'ass in pull' opening of doors

          today's   ah bit tree   arch

      where irised   my head   in stone

            an outer   'oss skull

      with martyred   lamb witch   bones

          anthers   no-nohing

           but the arc   off-oughts

    that start love-touched flesh   on dreams

          this unstrange   solidities

          how even   there

              ha sing visible   awes

iii) aurora revoice sin halo sits gold rinkered tether waltz meaning ass in pull opening of d'or studies ah bit tree arch wear irised mire din stone an out a 'oss skull whiff martyred lamb witch bones anther snow no wing but far cough oughts that start love touched flesh end reams this unstrange solid ditties how even the air ha sing visible lores

The Art of Divination

We've been talking about it for months:
through the stars, life's meanings, random

      stuff like Rumpelstiltskin, Monty Python,
      How was work? and *Did you swim?*

We shape text from the sounds
as if the space around were water

            supporting the words' tiny strokes
            towards a shore that grows closer.

We call ourselves good friends, frame
this ocean with hills as firm bookends.

        Only now and then, questions in silence
        cast loose between these steep slopes.

     Is it the shade of my shadows or yours
which tones the unspoken answers?

From Earth and Fire

Some Reunion

Long-time-no-see greets
ageing's short-term acquaintance
with a double-cheek kiss/hug/shy
coconut smile/shrugged grimace.
This twitch-eye/switch-hand/palm-
sweated/shared-footsy/knees-knocked/
eel-electric/skimmed-thigh re-meeting
is after large talk on small things
before morning pills swallowed,
with lushed sigh/rushed bye.
Sometimes, it's said later,
friendship never ends.

By Hand

To the margins, letters. On bleached bread,
knife spreading his daily butter. From
pockets, lifting loose coins. Over her head,
switching light. Under the bed, flinching
strayed socks. Below certainty, searching
her diary's doubted dates. Alongside
the phone, a strange voice uncoiling.
Through the open window, a passing
of glasses, nothing seeing. Through
the door, unlocking lateness, last-
minuted. Through her rush thoughts,
a scratching itch-flit. Beside a fleeting
hoped escape, the fridge's closing shush.
Out of her mind, knife-clutching…
To the|m|, |ar| gins|.| a|t| er|, |b |let|
s|on |b |leached |re|d |

Childbirth

When the sky splits,
he catches her red-handed,
nails night-stained, post-
storm taste on her breath,
streaks of pink violent in her hair.

He blunts the morning's pointed
start. Fingertips needle, twig-stitch
torn patches. As blue bruises,
he shoulders the horizon,
wears her skin in his branches.

A[gap]e

Candles flick flames where campfires
once patterned his face. Flesh lines
rested in medi(t)ation, shadows ash eyes.

From afar, breath disappears, sucked
into the days' hum; ribs in set ridges,
de-gusted. Draughts fill the gaps left

by words never heard. The only space
in the still-winged armchair is where
past happiness hides. Here, now s(t)ings.

On the Edge

the frost sun throws shadows
darkness slopes away

a log splinters red wood
fallen leaves scuffle

the hedgerow hoods barbed wire
shock of hard berries

distilled from quarried mist
'DEEP EXCAVATION'

crack of memory's twig hinge
cavitied stump

staring into steepness, jump
back from this hollow

where life falls in stone echoes
that moss gleanings won't soften

Between the Fir and the Brambles

She lusts for wild grass,
            wet lushness.
     But her husband, their neighbours...
She drags the mower out.
     Along their first border, the engine
            stops dead.
     She pulls a clot
from the rust, throws
     this at the bushes.
            Brambles grab and scratch.
     A dead frog drops
from the metal's
     dried blood.
            She brushes it aside,
     under the prickled
curve of red berries –
     clustered for a moment
            with her past
     hopes of princely kisses.
Then her husband's voice
     breaks the petrolled silence.
            She choke-starts
     the motor, scatters
its hacked harmonies
     across their uncut lawn.
            As she turns a corner,

the sudden perturbance of fir.
A screech of black feathers erupts.
Her sky bleeds green.

Unfoldings

He passes her the world's largest moth:
the Attacus Atlas, continents spanned
in its wings.
            Their mappings laid bare.
The wonder of paper shapes in his grasp.
That first origami! All the folded
light since. Dexterous hands revealed
humming birds, lilies, snakes' heads...

So many years from this here now.
He spins his globe, pinpoints origins,
then unstrings
            her spine again, twists loose
bones, plies skin to feathers, strips
flitting thoughts. His fingers coax her
past the white of duckling to swan.
Beyond the patterns of flight.

The (un)bespoken

Every whisper betrays
its doppelgangers – the caves
of like mouths,
where strange tongues' shadows
fall and rise
in a nerve-string puppetry.

That rushed escape
of caught breath on the moor,
this shush of gorse wind,
their splash of loosed water on stone,
gravity in torrents,
laughter shaken from a petal.

Life's repetitive looping:
sounds, senses, symbioses;
that spiralling slippage
between initial pulse – swifter
than wind, Iris-coloured –
and that synaptic spark crackle.

Each *I love you, I'm sorry, Not again!*
different and yet the same,
just as new spokes spin
thin air and cold metal,
or light unsilences old oil
in a rainbow against water.

Behind their many-wintered doors,

other lives guzzle dust. They roll away

from false pasts, and unlived futures:
morning skies dregged with red wine;

blown petals bumping elbows, stumbling
across frosted grass; the slip of wet mud,

broken-glass stones; discarded
sepal skirts mulched to lush soil.

Uncertainties heaped in restless rakings,
steeled tones digging forks and spades

into silenced darkness. Landscapes closed
with icicles, that numbness-curse crouching.

Cleaved from this deep-earthed uneasy,
the sh sh of moth-time, slowly unwrapping.

Warm breath evaporates traces of ice
from the world's scuffed, thin surface.

Visiting the Zoo

Drying her hands, the blowers
push flesh from bone in a mirage
of pulped skin ridges.

Imagine this then, a zebra loosing
its black and white pelt
amongst the floored paper towels.

How easy might it be to wrap
another's patterned shape around arms,
legs, torso, and walk out of here

as something else? Later,
dark hair feathers her fingers,
his breath skims her breasts.

She uncoils from the hotel bed
as serpent, ostrich and butterfly,
leaves the sheets as twisted chrysalis shreds.

Quarrying at Savage Hill

Stand away from the window –
you will not see her

moving through the long grass
to rest a hand on her quarry slab:

monument against Grandad's *God damn her*
and *What the hell d' you wan that fer?*

This was her garden, there is her stone,
here, finches in her fig tree.

Buttercups crow from the lawn,
daisies scatter, unmown.

Draw the curtains closed,
shut out this dust-laden light.

Limestone strengthens your spine,
her presence weaves within you.

After the Party

Someone stuffed the downed bottle
with screwed wrappers, sweets twisted
from their casings: a fish scale mosaic,
silvered skins scrunched. The gaps
– still lakes of air and glass distortion
around dead-gilled traces of party, fun,
life… All contorted to fill the shape
of emptiness; its gagged mouth,
throat, neck...space enough, just,
for the thin wax of one lit candle.

Solidity's Semblance

Y Ddraig Goch
fight the good fight
never surrender
solidity's semblance
one liquid
vibrations conjoined
flowing
mercy unstrained
knot of one substance
the heart's contractions fed
in canon with the lungs' expansion
undivided, let us sit
drinking from one bottle, vessel, body
into the world,
rejoicing

Composition

I lay on the forest floor to sleep.
Friends made me a pillow, a warm
swamping cover. My peat bed hardened.
Voices seeped my deep-coaled dreams.

Kershaw. Lower Yard. King. China. Pasture.

Bang! Shaken awake to dark rock,
muffled shouts, bells, that sulphur smell.
I felt myself fall; then jolt, judder, jolt…
a cranked jerk, lurched upwards.

Pasture-china-king-lower yard-kershaw.

The vibrations stopped. A hammer crack.
My iron bed split. Birdsong rushed in,
this fossil tale slipped out. Strangers
read the fern seeds in their palm.

Evening Blessing

Someone has drawn back the clouds,
unblinded the stratosphere. Even the gap
in the fence holds a plank of clear sky.

Evening peers through unknotted eyes.
Hundreds of leaves squint down as she whispers
to her son: *How quiet can you be? How still?*

Black-backed, they lie face up; limbs spread.
The trampoline sags only slightly beneath
the weight of their two flesh stars.

He twitches. She feels childhood itch;
breath disperse. Meshed light darkens.
Crimson seepage enfolds them.